Provinces and Territories of Canada

NEW
BRUNSWICK

— "Be … in this place" —

Published by Weigl Educational Publishers Limited
6325 10 Street SE
Calgary, Alberta
T2H 2Z9

www.weigl.com

Library and Archives Canada Cataloguing in Publication data available upon request.
Fax 403-233-7769 for the attention of the Publishing Records department.

ISBN 978-1-55388-983-0 (hard cover)
ISBN 978-1-55388-996-0 (soft cover)

Printed in the United States of America
1 2 3 4 5 6 7 8 9 0 13 12 11 10 09

Editor: Heather C. Hudak
Design: Terry Paulhus

Weigl acknowledges Getty Images as its primary image supplier for this title.
Brian Atkinson: pages 11 top, 24, 25 left, 33 bottom, 36, 37 middle, 37 bottom, 40, 41, 42 top; Canadian War Museum: page 38 bottom; Gérard Sirois: pages 35 top, 35 middle; J.F. Bergeron: page 23 top; National Archives of Canada: page 26 bottom, 26 top, 27 top, 27 bottom, 38 top; Provincial Archives of New Brunswick: page 25 right; T. Clifford Hodgson: page 19 top; Theatre New Brunswick: page 39 right.

We gratefully acknowledge the financial support of the Government of Canada through the Book Publishing Industry Development Program (BPIDP) for our publishing activities.

Contents

New Brunswick 4

Land and Climate 8

Natural Resources 10

Plants and Animals........................12

Tourism 16

Industry 18

Goods and Services........................20

First Nations 24

Explorers 26

Early Settlers 28

Population........................32

Politics and Government 34

Cultural Groups 36

Arts and Entertainment........................38

Sports 40

Canada 44

Brain Teasers 46

More Information........................47

Index 48

New Brunswick

N ew Brunswick is nicknamed the "Picture Province" because of its long and beautiful coastlines, rugged hills, lush forests, many rivers and lakes, and charming towns and cities. The province boasts a rich and colourful heritage that can be seen in its many historical buildings, monuments, and cultural celebrations. New Brunswick is located in Atlantic Canada and is the largest of the three Maritime Provinces. Nova Scotia and Prince Edward Island are the other two. They are called Maritime Provinces because each is bordered by water on at least three sides.

New Brunswick ranks eighth in size among the Canadian provinces.

New Brunswick is known for its many covered bridges.

N ew Brunswick acts as a gateway province. It provides transportation links to other parts of Atlantic Canada. Quebec borders New Brunswick to the north, but the Restigouche River and Chaleur Bay also form part of the northern border. The U.S. state of Maine borders the west of New Brunswick, and the Gulf of Saint Lawrence and the Northumberland Strait form the eastern border. Part of New Brunswick's southern border consists of Chignecto Bay and the **Isthmus** of Chignecto, a 24-kilometre wide piece of land that connects the province to Nova Scotia. The rest of the southern border is occupied by the Bay of Fundy.

New Brunswick's landscape is as rich and fascinating as its cultural heritage. Forests cover most of the land, providing great opportunities for outdoor enthusiasts to enjoy many activities, including hiking, cycling, and cross-country skiing. New Brunswick's forests are also home to a wide variety of wildlife. There are two national parks in the province. Fundy National Park has a spectacular coastline and a bay that

The Bouctouche region, in southeastern New Brunswick, has long stretches of shoreline that attract tourists year round.

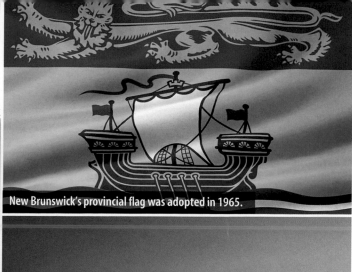

New Brunswick's provincial flag was adopted in 1965.

Fredericton is the capital city of New Brunswick.

has the world's largest tides. The wild water has also carved out some unusual shapes in the rugged rocks that line the coast. These fascinating rocks can be seen at low tide. Kouchibouguac National Park, which runs along the Northumberland Strait, is less rugged than Fundy National Park, but just as beautiful. It is mostly flat, with sand dunes, calm shores, and long, beautiful beaches. Visitors from all over Canada as well as other countries come to New Brunswick to enjoy its beaches and to take in the spectacular scenery of the parks.

New Brunswick has many rivers. The Saint John River is the longest and flows north to south in the western part of the province. Other major rivers include the Petitcodiac, the Miramichi, the Restigouche, and the Nepisiguit.

The entire eastern border of New Brunswick is coastal. It has the warmest salt water north of Virginia.

Kouchibouguac National Park is the largest park in New Brunswick. It encompasses about 240 square kilometres of wilderness.

Saint John and Dalhousie are New Brunswick's main seaports.

New Brunswick was named in honour of England's King George III, who also served as the Duke of Brunswick.

The provincial motto is *spem reduxit,* which means "hope was restored."

Chaleur Bay was named for its warm waters. Chaleur means "warmth" in French.

Many people in New Brunswick dress in the colours of the Acadian flag during the various Acadian festivals that are held in the province.

LAND AND CLIMATE

New Brunswick has a fascinating and varied landscape. The interior of the province is mostly rolling **plateaus** covered almost completely by forests. The southern terrain is more rugged. Just a few kilometres north of the Bay of Fundy, there are steep hills running east to west. Steep, rugged hills also dominate the north-central part of New Brunswick. The magnificent Saint John River splits the province from north to south. It is an impressive 673 kilometres long. New Brunswick also boasts numerous lakes. Grand Lake, east of Fredericton, is the largest.

The seasons in New Brunswick are very well-defined. Winters are snowy and cold. Summers are warm and pleasant. Temperatures range from an extreme low of –37° Celsius in winter to an extreme high of 37° Celsius in summer. On average, the temperature in January is –9° Celsius, and in July, it is about 19° Celsius. Temperatures are more moderate in the southern coastal regions. Normal annual rainfall in New Brunswick is 825 millimetres. Normal annual snowfall is about 2,900 millimetres.

Mount Carleton Provincial Park is home to a number of impressive uplands, including its namesake. Mount Carleton is the highest point in the province, at 820 metres.

It is common for many of New Brunswick's rivers to flood in the spring.

Northwestern New Brunswick receives the largest amount of snow in the province.

Autumn in New Brunswick consists of cold nights and warm days, turning the leaves vibrant colours that contrast with the dark evergreen trees.

KEEP CONNECTED
The New Brunswick Forest Products Association website has a great deal of information about the province's forestry industry. Visit the site at **http://nbforestry.com.**

New Brunswick's trees are an important natural resource. Forestry employs more than 16,000 people in the province. Several towns and cities, mostly in the northern part of the province, depend on large pulp and paper mills as their major employers. The forests supply the materials for many products including lumber, plywood, and fuel.

Fish are another important natural resource for New Brunswick. There are more than 50 species of fish found in the province's waters. Lobster, scallops, herring, cod, and mackerel make up the bulk of the catch. New Brunswick also has rich mineral deposits. Zinc, potash, copper, lead, silver, and **antimony** are just some of the minerals found throughout the province.

The New Brunswick Mining and Mineral Interpretation Centre is located in Petit-Rocher. It promotes the province's mining heritage.

New Brunswick's spruce trees are major contributors to the province's pulp industry. Wood pulp is one of New Brunswick's most valuable manufactured products.

GET THE FACTS

The world's largest species of tuna, the bluefin, is found in New Brunswick's waters. Most of the bluefin catch is exported to Japan.

Bathurst, in the northeast of the province, is home to some of the world's largest zinc mines.

New Brunswick is one of the country's major producers of antimony. This mineral is used in medicines, matches, and fire-proofing materials.

PLANTS AND ANIMALS

About half of New Brunswick's forests are mixed with hardwoods and softwoods. Spruce and fir are the most dominant softwoods in these forests, while maple trees are the most dominant hardwoods.

The purple violet was adopted as New Brunswick's flower in 1936, at the request of the provincial Women's Institute.

New Brunswick is one of the most densely forested regions in the world. Forests cover about 85 percent of the province. Spruce, fir, and tamarack are the most common trees within New Brunswick's northern forests. Mixed forests, with maple, birch, and pine trees, can be found along the Restigouche River and near Chaleur Bay. The Acadian mixed forest can be found in the southern and eastern parts of the province. This forest is made up of several tree species, including sugar maple, birch, white pine, fir, and hemlock.

Trees and plant life abound in every region of the province. Wild cranberries and blueberries grow in the southwest, and the northeast coast has peat bogs. These bogs are damp, muddy areas where dead plant matter has been **compressed** over the centuries into a dark layer called peat. Peat can be cut into bricks, dried, and burned for fuel.

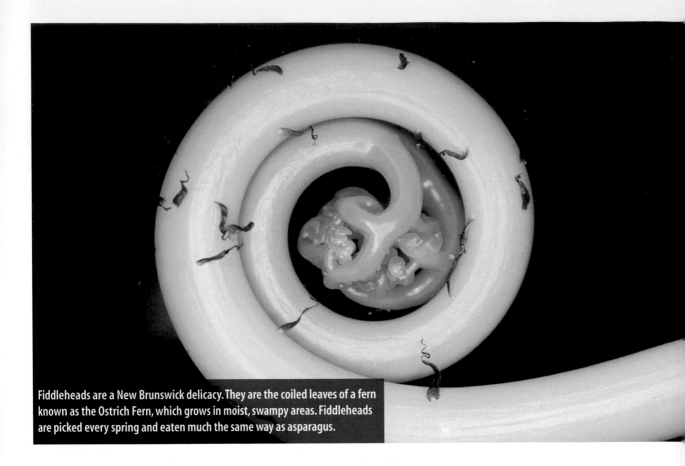

Fiddleheads are a New Brunswick delicacy. They are the coiled leaves of a fern known as the Ostrich Fern, which grows in moist, swampy areas. Fiddleheads are picked every spring and eaten much the same way as asparagus.

Dulse is a tasty seaweed that grows in the province. Most of the dulse eaten in North America is gathered just off the New Brunswick coast, in the Bay of Fundy. During low tide, long strands of dulse are hand-picked from between rocks. It is then dried and packed for shipment to markets all over North America.

New Brunswick's vast forests are home to a wide assortment of wildlife. Among the larger animals living in the forests are moose, black bears, wildcats, and white-tailed deer. Smaller animals include muskrats, martens, minks, rabbits, skunks, and squirrels.

Hundreds of different birds also live in New Brunswick. Partridges, pheasants, and woodcocks can all be seen in many of the province's open areas. Geese and ducks are also common sights. Mary's Point, in Fundy

KEEP CONNECTED
To learn more about fiddleheads, surf to **www.thecanadianencyclopedia.com**. Type the word "fiddleheads" into the search engine, and click on the first story.

American lobsters live in New Brunswick's coastal waters. They live at the bottom of the sea, usually at depths of 3 metres, but they can be found as deep as 720 metres.

The official bird of New Brunswick is the black-capped chickadee. It was named the provincial bird in August 1983 after a contest was conducted by the provincial Federation of Naturalists.

National Park, is one of the best places to see the thousands of sandpipers and plovers that gather on the **mudflats** to eat tiny shrimps and worms. Seabirds, including the increasingly rare puffin, nest in colonies on some coastal islands.

The province also has a large assortment of marine life. Several rivers in New Brunswick are known for their Atlantic salmon, white trout, bass, and pickerel. Lobsters, clams, oysters, sardines, cod, and herring can all be found in the province's coastal waters.

GET THE FACTS

Puffins feed on fish. They face a potential food shortage because of intense commercial fishing in their home waters.

Black bears wander throughout New Brunswick's forests in search of food sources. They hibernate for five to seven months each year.

The two best times to see migrating birds in New Brunswick are early spring and late summer.

More than 15 species of whales can be seen near the western islands of the Bay of Fundy. Seals and porpoises also live in the Bay of Fundy.

TOURISM

There is a lot to see and do in New Brunswick. Athletic tourists will enjoy sea kayaking, mountain climbing, hiking, camping, and fishing. Art and history enthusiasts can tour the province's historical settlements, museums, and art galleries.

One of the biggest attractions in New Brunswick is Fundy National Park. The tides in the Bay of Fundy are the highest and the wildest in the world. The water rises and falls the height of a four-storey building. Twice a day, the incoming tide is so powerful that it forces the Saint John River, which flows into the sea, to flow backwards.

East Quoddy Lighthouse on Campobello Island is one of the oldest lighthouses in Canada.

Low tide at the Bay of Fundy's Hopewell Rocks reveals striking rock formations.

Also in the Bay of Fundy are the Fundy Isles—Deer Island, Campobello, and Grand Manan. Writers and painters have used Grand Manan as a retreat for years. Campobello was the site of the summer home of former United States President Franklin D. Roosevelt.

A popular tourist site is the giant lobster in Shediac, the lobster capital of the world.

The Fairmont Algonquin Hotel is located in St. Andrews by the Sea.

GET THE FACTS

Magnetic Hill, in Moncton, is a natural attraction that draws tourists from all over the world. Visitors simply put their car in neutral at the foot of the hill, and watch in wonder as an optical illusion makes it seem as though they are rolling backwards up the hill. Even water seems to flow uphill at this natural wonder.

Doll enthusiasts will love Delia's Dollhouse in Petitcodiac. It is home to more than 4,000 dolls of different sizes, shapes, and brands. Visitors to the museum will see dolls from around the world, dressed for all seasons.

INDUSTRY

The construction industry employs thousands of people in the province. It contributes about $1 billion to the economy each year.

New Brunswick's forests are the economic backbone of the province. Forestry brings in about $2 billion every year—pulp production is valued at $1.5 billion a year, and solid wood products account for $500 million. Eastern New Brunswick is an important centre for the pulp and paper industry, while the northern part of the province has a highly developed lumber industry. New Brunswick is also considered a leader in forest management.

Fishing is another important industry in the province. Commercial fishing is carried out all along New Brunswick's coastline, and employs about 7,000 fishers and 12,000 plant workers. The province also raises fish and shellfish in **hatcheries**. This industry is called **aquaculture**. With the threat of reduced catches in traditional fishing, aquaculture is rapidly becoming an important activity in New Brunswick. Hatcheries in the province produce many fish and shellfish, including salmon, trout, mussels, and oysters.

Agriculture also plays a large role in New Brunswick's economy. Potatoes are the leading **cash crop**—the income from potato sales alone accounts for about 22 percent of the province's farming income.

Fishing is a major industry in New Brunswick.

Most of New Brunswick's potato farms are located in the upper Saint John River Valley, in the counties of Carleton and Victoria.

GET THE FACTS

The mining industry plays a major role in the provincial economy. It employs about 4,000 people and earns about $1 billion a year.

The Musée Acadien is located at the Université de Moncton.

In the early 1800s, logging was the mainstay of New Brunswick's economy. Most of the wood was used for shipbuilding.

Tourism is another major industry in New Brunswick. Well over one million tourists visit the province every year.

New Brunswick leads the country in military shipbuilding.

There are about 400 potato farms in the province.

GOODS AND SERVICES

Some of the finest maple syrup produced in North America comes from New Brunswick.

Seed potatoes are planted in the ground and used to grow potato plants.

New Brunswick's farms produce a variety of goods. Seed potatoes grown in the province are exported to over 30 countries around the world. The province's fresh fruit, including strawberries, blueberries, and apples, is also distributed elsewhere. Most of New Brunswick's remaining agricultural products, such as vegetables and dairy products, are consumed within the province.

A variety of goods are manufactured in New Brunswick, including wood pulp, paper, metal products, transportation equipment, and plastic products. Food production is the leader in New Brunswick's manufacturing industry. Fish, potatoes, vegetables, dairy products, and meats are all processed in the province. Many of New Brunswick's manufactured goods are exported via the port facilities at Saint John.

Many of New Brunswick's locally-grown and manufactured goods are sold at farmers' markets throughout the province.

Many people in New Brunswick work in the service industry. Some service trades include jobs in banks, hospitals, insurance companies, and retail stores. The tourism industry is also a service-provider, and many residents in New Brunswick work in hotels, restaurants, or at various tourist attractions.

Education is another important service. New Brunswick has a provincially-funded public education system, which offers instruction in both French and English. The province is also home to four public universities—the University of New Brunswick, with campuses in Fredericton and Saint John; Saint Thomas University, in Fredericton; Mount Allison University, in Sackville; and Université de Moncton, in the city of Moncton, with smaller campuses in Edmundston and Shippegan.

The University of New Brunswick was founded in 1785. Today, about 10,000 students attend the multi-campus school.

Each institution offers students a wide range of learning opportunities, and each has its own unique features. The University of New Brunswick is the oldest English-language university in Canada, and the Université de Moncton is the country's largest francophone institution outside of Quebec. The province is also home to New Brunswick Community College, which offers many different learning and training programs.

There are 11 television stations and 37 radio stations in the province.

New Brunswick generates an enormous amount of electricity. This has created a **surplus** of power, allowing the province to export its excess electricity to neighbouring provinces and to the United States.

New Brunswick has five daily newspapers—four in English and one in French. The English dailies include *The Daily Gleaner*, from Fredericton; the *Telegraph-Journal* from Saint John; and the *Times & Transcript*, from Moncton. The French newspaper is *L'Acadie Nouvelle*, published in Caraquet and Moncton.

New Brunswick is interconnected with electrical utilities in Quebec, Nova Scotia, and Prince Edward Island.

The only nuclear power plant in the Atlantic provinces is located in New Brunswick.

FIRST NATIONS

Today, the Mi'kmaq preserve their traditional ways of life by passing them on to younger generations.

Two Aboriginal groups lived in the New Brunswick region long before any European settlers arrived. These groups were the Maliseet and the Mi'kmaq. Each had a distinct language and occupied a distinct territory. The Maliseet lived mostly in the Saint John River Valley. The Mi'kmaq traditionally occupied the area around the Gulf of Saint Lawrence and the Northumberland Strait, on the eastern side of the province.

KEEP CONNECTED

A Micmac Experience at the Bouctouche First Nation provides visitors with information about the traditionals ways of life of the Mi'kmaq. To learn more about this experience, visit **http://mediaroom. acoa-apeca.gc.ca/e/media/press/press.shtml?836.**

Esgenoôpetitj First Nation holds an annual powwow.

During the World Wars, many Mi'kmaq and Maliseet men served in the armed forces.

Both the Maliseet and Mi'kmaq hunted and fished. When the first Europeans arrived, trade developed between the Aboriginal Peoples and the new settlers. The Aboriginal Peoples traded fish, fur, snowshoes, and canoes in exchange for copper kettles, iron knives, and firearms.

GET THE FACTS

The Mi'kmaq did not live in permanent villages. They moved from place to place, depending on the seasons.

Many Maliseet farmed in the New Brunswick area. They worked the soil and made their own farm tools.

The Mi'kmaq would sometimes use torches to hunt birds and fish. The bright light of the torch would attract the prey, making them flock around it. Hunters could then spear the fish, or knock the birds from the sky with clubs.

EXPLORERS

The first European explorer to New Brunswick was a Frenchman named Jacques Cartier. He sailed through the area in 1534, and claimed the land for France. He did not, however, stay there for long.

Champlain paved the way for future settlements on New France's land. Before fertile land was farmed, settlers cleared the area of trees.

In 1603, the King of France sent Samuel de Champlain and Pierre du Gua de Monts to the Maritimes to explore and settle the region. Their ships entered the mouth of a large river, the Saint Croix, on June 14, 1604. These men, along with several other French settlers, spent the winter at the mouth of the Saint Croix River, but moved on to establish a settlement in the Nova Scotia region in 1605. The French named the whole Atlantic region "Acadia."

Jacques Cartier sailed from St. Malo, France, in 1534.

Champlain recognized the need to use Aboriginal Peoples' methods of transportation and their knowledge and assistance at navigating New France's land.

Vikings may have been the first Europeans to see New Brunswick's shores from their longships as early as the 11th century.

Champlain's wife, Hélène Boullé, often taught Huron children in the Quebec settlement. After Champlain's death, Hélène became a nun.

Jacques Cartier was trying to find a sea passage around North America to Asia when he sailed along the northern shore of New Brunswick in 1534.

Samuel de Champlain almost died during the first winter on Saint Croix because he could not cross the water to the mainland to get more food and resources.

Samuel de Champlain was hired by Pierre du Gua de Monts to be the cartographer on the journey to the Maritimes.

A MAP of the
INHABITED PART
OF
CANADA,
from the French Surveys; with
the FRONTIERS of
NEW YORK and NEW ENGLAND,
from the Large Survey
By CLAUDE JOSEPH SAUTHIER.
Engraved by Wᵐ FADEN, 1777.

Many settlers came to what is now Canada to take part in the fur trade.

The Treaty of Utrecht was signed between the queen of Great Britain and the king of France.

In the late 1600s, French settlers arrived and established farms and fishing stations throughout Acadia. Many of these settlers hoped to develop a strong fur trade and soon began to fight for control of the territory. This competition gradually settled down, only to be replaced by a rivalry between the French and the British settlers. The British had colonies in the area that were becoming large and powerful.

The Acadian settlers were caught in the struggle between the French and British over control of the Atlantic region. Many battles took place during this power struggle. In 1713, France lost most of its Acadian land to Britain in the **Treaty** of Utrecht. The region became a British colony.

After the Treaty of Paris, many of the expelled Acadians returned and built new settlements.

The British feared that the Acadians living in this area would side with the French in any future wars, and tried to persuade the Acadians to pledge **allegiance** to the British king. The Acadians just wanted to be left alone to farm and live in peace. In 1755, when another war was about to break out between the French and the British, thousands of Acadians were **expelled** from the area.

In 1783, there was a major increase in the population of the Maritimes. This increase was a result of the **American Revolution**, which was fought between Britain and its 13 American colonies from 1755 to 1783. The war ended when Britain granted the American colonies their independence. However, there were many people in these colonies who wanted to remain loyal to the British crown. These people were called Loyalists, and after the war, many of them fled to Canada.

In 1785, due to the massive number of Loyalists who had settled in the area, Saint John was incorporated as Canada's first city. It has always been the largest city in New Brunswick.

When the Acadians were expelled in 1755, some escaped to what was then the uninhabited coastline along the Gulf of Saint Lawrence and Chaleur Bay. Today, that area is known as the Acadian Peninsula.

About 14,000 Loyalists settled in the Saint John Valley area. This was such a large number that in 1784, the settlement, which was considered part of Nova Scotia, became a separate colony. It was named New Brunswick.

Settlers continued to arrive in New Brunswick. In the early 1800s, many Scottish and Irish people came to the area. In 1870, a few hundred Danes arrived in the colony and settled in Victoria Country. As the 19th century drew to a close, settlement in the area declined.

GET THE FACTS

In 1763, France, through the Treaty of Paris, gave up all its lands in North America to Britain. However, it was agreed that the French-speaking people of Acadia would be allowed to continue to practise their own traditions, speak their own language, have their own schools, and practise their own religion.

So many Loyalists settled in the New Brunswick area that the province was sometimes referred to as "The Loyalist Province."

Some Loyalists brought their houses on **barges** to establish communities in New Brunswick.

POPULATION

About 729,997 people live in New Brunswick. Most people live along the coast and in the river valleys. Saint John is the province's oldest and largest city, with a population of about 122,389. The next most populated city is Moncton with approximately 64,128 people, followed by Fredericton, the capital, with about 50,535 people.

New Brunswick is Canada's only officially bilingual province. About 70 percent of the population speaks English, and 30 percent speaks French. The English-speaking majority is made up largely of descendants of the Scottish, Irish, and English settlers of the 18th and 19th centuries. These descendants live mostly in the southern and western parts of the province.

There are seven cities, 28 towns, and 68 villages in New Brunswick.

The French-speaking minority lives mostly in the northern and eastern regions and consists of the descendants of early Acadian settlers as well as French Canadians from Quebec. Today, Acadians live mostly in small communities in the northeastern part of the province. These small French communities maintain their heritage with many festivals and celebrations.

Moncton, in the southeast of the province, developed into a railroad and distribution centre in the late nineteenth century.

The American Loyalists of the 18th century had a major effect on the development of New Brunswick. Many of these people came to New Brunswick in order to maintain their British loyalty and begin a new life. Today, descendants of these early settlers continue to live in the province and celebrate their heritage with fairs and historic re-enactments. There are also strong Irish, Scottish, and Danish roots in New Brunswick.

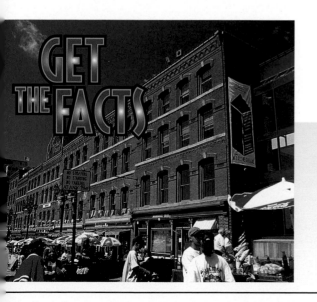

GET THE FACTS

Market Square, in Saint John, is a popular gathering place, especially during the warm, summer months.

It is common practice for New Brunswickers to commute to the cities from rural or suburban areas.

In the 20th century, small numbers of eastern European, Dutch, German, Italian, and South and East Asian immigrants settled in the larger cities in New Brunswick.

POLITICS AND GOVERNMENT

Property services such as streetlights, sewers, and recreation are the responsibility of the local government.

New Brunswick's provincial government is responsible for many social services, including education, housing, health, and justice. The Provincial Legislature is located in the capital city of Fredericton. There are 58 members in the province's Legislative Assembly. Each member represents a **constituency** and is elected by the public. The political party with the most elected members forms the provincial government, and the leader of that party becomes the premier. The premier then appoints a Cabinet, consisting of twenty members from the Legislative Assembly. Each member of the Cabinet heads a different provincial department.

New Brunswick is represented in Canada's federal government by 10 provincially elected members in the House of Commons and 10 appointed seats in the Canadian Senate. There are also three types of local government in the province—municipal, local service district, and rural communities. Municipal governments administer New Brunswick's cities, towns, and villages.

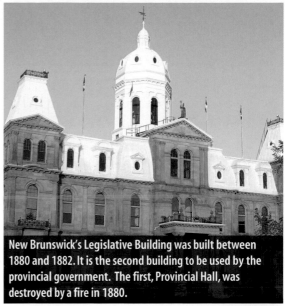

New Brunswick's Legislative Building was built between 1880 and 1882. It is the second building to be used by the provincial government. The first, Provincial Hall, was destroyed by a fire in 1880.

People can take guided tours of Old Government House in Fredericton.

Only Liberals and Progressive Conservatives have formed governments in New Brunswick. The New Democratic Party established a small following in the late 20th century.

Areas with small populations in the province are administered by 272 local service districts.

A large French-speaking community lives in the Madawaska region, which is situated in the northwest part of the province. Edmundston is considered the capital of the "Republic of Madawaska." This symbolic republic was created by the people of the region who, tired of border disputes between Canada and the United States, decided to form an independent country.

The Republic of Madawaska has its own flag—an eagle in a semi-circle of six stars.

New Brunswick was one of the four original provinces to make up Confederation in 1867. The others were Ontario, Quebec, and Nova Scotia.

Each member of New Brunswick's Legislative Assembly serves a five-year term.

CULTURAL GROUPS

New Brunswick is home to many different cultural groups that work to maintain the traditions and heritage of their ancestors. Acadians live mostly in the region known as the Acadian Peninsula. The people of the region celebrate and share their heritage through festivals, museums, and various historical sites. The town of Caraquet is often considered the centre of Acadian culture. Each year, it hosts the Acadian Festival. Events at the festival include dances, plays, parades, and the famous blessing of the fishing fleet. Caraquet is also home to the Acadian Museum and the Sainte-Anne-du-Bocage Shrine, which honours the area's earliest Acadian settlers.

Acadians also share their heritage at the Acadian Historical Village, just outside of Caraquet. This village shows how Acadians lived between the years 1780 and 1880. This was the period when many returned from exile to rebuild their lives in New Brunswick. Visitors to the village can see authentic Acadian buildings, including a church, a school, a printing house, and a general store. People dressed in period costumes give demonstrations on many different aspects of traditional Acadian living, including farming, weaving, and spinning.

Many descendants of New Brunswick's Loyalist settlers still call the province home. A large number of these descendants live in the city of Saint John.

Acadians in New Brunswick celebrate their culture with many annual festivals. Among them is the Caraquet Acadian Festival, which draws large crowds and lasts for ten days.

The Loyalist Heritage Festival in Saint John celebrates the arrival of the Loyalist settlers. The festival is held every year in mid-July. Parades, horse racing, and an antique fair are all part of the celebration.

Saint John is also home to the Loyalist House and the New Brunswick Museum, both of which house many Loyalist artifacts. King's Landing Historical Settlement, near Fredericton, has several fully furnished and functional traditional Loyalist homes for visitors to explore. Saint John is also known as Canada's most Irish city. Descendants of New Brunswick's earliest Irish settlers, along with more recent Irish immigrants, celebrate their heritage in many ways. There is a week-long celebration of Saint Patrick's Day in Saint John, and the city of Miramichi hosts "Canada's Irish Festival" every July. This is the oldest and largest Irish festival in the country, and it features pipe bands, Irish games, films, and crafts.

The Scottish are a prominent cultural group in New Brunswick. The Highland Society at Miramichi was founded in 1842. The society celebrates its Scottish heritage with the annual Highland Gathering each August.

Acadians have their own flag and anthem, which were chosen at the Acadian convention of 1884. August 15 is the date of the official Acadian holiday.

Employees at King's Landing Historical Settlement dress in period costumes and demonstrate traditional methods of farming and cooking.

ARTS AND ENTERTAINMENT

Many talented writers have drawn upon New Brunswick's people and landscapes for inspiration. Antonine Maillet was born in Bouctouche and has written more than 30 works, many of which have won literary awards. Perhaps her most famous story is La Sagouine, the legend of an Acadian scrubwoman. A number of famous poets, including Bliss Carman and Sir Charles G.D.

One of the most well-known art galleries in New Brunswick is the Beaverbrook Art Gallery, in Fredericton. Among its many exhibits is a small collection of British painting from the last three centuries.

Roberts, are also from New Brunswick. Fredericton is often called "The Poets Corner of Canada." It is home to *The Fiddlehead* at the University of New Brunswick.

Many visual artists have also come from New Brunswick. Miller Brittain and Jack Humphrey are from Saint John. Both men were known for their

Alex Colville worked as an official war artist during World War II. One of his best-known works from the war was *Infantry near Nijmegen, Holland.* Two of Alex Colville's pupils, Christopher Pratt and Thomas Forrestall, are well-known for their paintings of eastern Canada.

depictions of war and the Depression. Mount Allison University is known for producing great visual artists, particularly between 1946 and 1963, when Alex Colville taught there. Alex Colville is considered one of Canada's leading painters.

New Brunswick has an active music scene. A number of regional and provincial music festivals are held throughout the year. Among the most popular music festivals are the Lamèque International Festival of **Baroque** Music and the Miramichi Folksong Festival. The Baroque festival is held on the island of Lameque in mid-July. It celebrates composers like Vivaldi, Scarlatti, and Bach. Concerts are held in a church that has some of the finest **acoustics** in the country. The Miramichi Folksong Festival is held every summer and features singers, step-dancers, fiddlers, and folk musicians.

This production, entitled *Gaze*, was an original play put on by Theatre New Brunswick. Along with performing plays, Theatre New Brunswick also hosts theatre camps for children.

The theatre scene is also active in New Brunswick. Fredericton's Theatre New Brunswick produces original and classical plays as well as musicals. The company tours many of the province's cities and towns. The Université de Moncton has its own theatre group, which produces plays in French.

Bilingual pop star Roch Voisine is from Edmundston.

GET THE FACTS

New Brunswick has produced a couple of country music singing sensations: Chris Cummings is from Norton, and Julian Austin is from Saint John.

Fiddlehead is Canada's oldest literary magazine.

The Festival international du cinéma francophone en Acadie is an annual film festival that focusses on French films from France, Belgium, Africa, and Canada. It takes place in Moncton every September.

So many poets have either lived or worked in New Brunswick that it is often called "The Poetry Province."

Acadian singer Edith Butler, born in Paquetville in 1942, is popular internationally with 15 albums to her credit.

Many sport fishers head to the Miramichi and Restigouche Rivers in the hope of catching a mighty Atlantic salmon. However, in order to conserve the threatened population, these fishers must release the salmon they catch.

New Brunswick's many scenic lakes make canoeing a very popular activity in the province. An organization called "Canoe New Brunswick" offers canoe and kayaking courses.

New Brunswick's extensive wilderness provides plenty of opportunity for outdoor recreation. In the summer, people can hike, cycle, bird-watch, or camp in Fundy National Park or Kouchibouguac National Park. Water sports are also popular. People can swim, sail, windsurf, and kayak. White-water rafting over some of the province's wild rapids is another exciting pastime. New Brunswick's waters also attract a number of fishers.

There are more than 40 golf courses in New Brunswick.

The province has several activities to enjoy during the winter. Cross-country skiing and downhill skiing are popular in the northern part of New Brunswick. Sugarloaf Provincial Park, in Atholville, offers nine alpine ski runs, as well as snowmobile and snowshoeing trails. Visitors to Sugarloaf can also toboggan on a steep hill or skate on a natural pond. Hockey and curling are other favourite winter sports among many New Brunswickers.

There are no major league sports teams in New Brunswick, yet many excellent athletes come from the province. The New Brunswick Sports Hall of Fame, in Fredericton, pays tribute to many of these athletes. There are approximately 8,000 pieces of memorabilia which

Matt Stairs is a player with the Philadelphia Phillies. He was born in Saint John in 1968.

One of the most popular beaches in the province is Parlee Beach, at Pointe-du-Chene.

commemorate New Brunswick's sporting history. Among the athletes honoured at the museum are Olympic medallist Marianne Limpert and legendary jockey Ron Turcotte.

New Brunswick is home to a number of impressive amateur sports teams. The province has four teams in the Maritime Junior A Hockey League, including the Dieppe Gagnon Commandos, the Woodstock Slammers, the Miramichi Timberwolves, and the Campbellton Jr. A Tigers.

GET THE FACTS

Whale watching has become a favourite pastime. Humpback whales are most commonly seen. People can watch these magnificent creatures swimming in the Bay of Fundy and the Gulf of Saint Lawrence.

In 1999, Saint John became an international stage for the Sun Life Skate Canada figure skating championships.

Rheal Cormier is a Major League Baseball pitcher. He was born in Moncton in 1967.

CANADA

Canada is a vast nation, and each province and territory has its own unique features. This map shows important information about each of Canada's 10 provinces and three territories, including when they joined Confederation, their size, population, and capital city. For more information about Canada, visit **http://canada.gc.ca**.

Alberta
Entered Confederation: 1905
Capital: Edmonton
Area: 661,848 sq km
Population: 3,632,483

British Columbia
Entered Confederation: 1871
Capital: Victoria
Area: 944,735 sq km
Population: 4,419,974

Manitoba
Entered Confederation: 1870
Capital: Winnipeg
Area: 647,797 sq km
Population: 1,213,815

New Brunswick
Entered Confederation: 1867
Capital: Fredericton
Area: 72,908 sq km
Population: 748,319

Newfoundland and Labrador
Entered Confederation: 1949
Capital: St. John's
Area: 405,212 sq km
Population: 508,990

SYMBOLS OF NEW BRUNSWICK

FLAG

COAT OF ARMS

FLOWER
Purple Violet

Map labels

Alert
smere
land

Baffin Bay

0   200   400 Kilometers
0   200   400 Miles

Baffin
Island

Davis Strait

Iqaluit
(Frobisher Bay)

Ivujivik

Labrador
Sea

dson
Bay

NEWFOUNDLAND

Schefferville

Happy Valley-
Goose Bay

Island of
Newfoundland

Chisasibi
(Fort George)

Gander
Saint John's

QUEBEC   Sept-Iles

Gulf of

Moosonee

St. Lawrence

St. Pierre and
Miquelon (FRANCE)

Chibougamau

PRINCE
EDWARD
ISLAND

Sydney

Quebec

NEW
BRUNSWICK

Charlottetown

Fredericton

Sherbrooke

Saint
John

Halifax

Sudbury   Montreal

NOVA
SCOTIA

Ottawa

Lake
Huron

Toronto
Hamilton
London

Lake
Ontario

Lake Erie

ANIMAL
Black-capped Chickadee

TREE
Balsam Fir

Northwest Territories
Entered Confederation: 1870
Capital: Yellowknife
Area: 1,346,106 sq km
Population: 42,940

Nova Scotia
Entered Confederation: 1867
Capital: Halifax
Area: 55,284 sq km
Population: 939,531

Nunavut
Entered Confederation: 1999
Capital: Iqaluit
Area: 2,093,190 sq km
Population: 531,556

Ontario
Entered Confederation: 1867
Capital: Toronto
Area: 1,076,395 sq km
Population: 12,986,857

Prince Edward Island
Entered Confederation: 1873
Capital: Charlottetown
Area: 5,660 sq km
Population: 140,402

Quebec
Entered Confederation: 1867
Capital: Quebec City
Area: 1,542,056 sq km
Population: 7,782,561

Saskatchewan
Entered Confederation: 1905
Capital: Regina
Area: 651,036 sq km
Population: 1,023,810

Yukon
Entered Confederation: 1898
Capital: Whitehorse
Area: 482,443 sq km
Population: 33,442

BRAIN TEASERS

Test your knowledge of New Brunswick by trying to answer these boggling brain teasers!

1 Multiple Choice

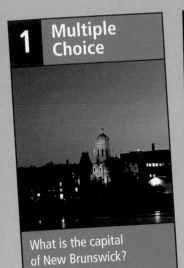

What is the capital of New Brunswick?
a) Miramichi
b) Saint John
c) Fredericton
d) Moncton

2 True or False?

New Brunswick is Canada's only official bilingual province.

3 Multiple Choice

Which of the following is NOT an important natural resource in New Brunswick?
a) lumber
b) oil
c) minerals
d) fish

4 True or False?

New Brunswick has several major league sports teams.

5 Multiple Choice

What is New Brunswick's leading cash crop?
a) wheat
b) cucumbers
c) potatoes
d) canola

6 Multiple Choice

What percent of New Brunswickers are French speakers?
a) 90
c) 50
d) 30
e) 5

7 True or False?

New Brunswick leads Canada in military shipbuilding.

8 Multiple Choice

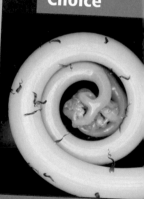

What are fiddleheads?
a) a type of flowering tree
b) the coiled leaves of a fern
c) a type of singing bird
d) a type of edible grass

1. c, Fredericton is the capital of New Brunswick. 2. True 3. b, Oil is not a natural resource in New Brunswick. 4. False, New Brunswick has no major league sports teams. 5. c, Potatoes are New Brunswick's leading cash crop. 6. c, 30 percent of New Brunswickers are French speakers. 7. True 8. b, Fiddleheads are the coiled leaves of a fern.

MORE INFORMATION

GLOSSARY

acoustics: designed for controlling and enhancing the quality of sound

allegiance: loyalty to a government or ruler

American Revolution: the war between Great Britain and its American colonies, lasting from 1775 to 1785

antimony: a metallic-white element

aquaculture: fish farming

barges: flat-bottomed boats used to transport goods and people

baroque: a style of music from the period 1600–1750

cash crop: a crop that sells well

compressed: flattened by pressure

constituency: voters or residents in a designated district

expelled: driven out or forced away

hatcheries: places for hatching eggs

isthmus: a narrow strip of land with water on either side, linking two larger areas of land

mudflats: stretches of land covered in mud from advancing and retreating tidal waters

plateaus: raised stretches of land with relatively level surfaces

surplus: an amount greater than what is needed

treaty: a formal agreement

BOOKS

Sarich, Leah. *Canada's Land and People: New Brunswick*. Calgary: Weigl Educational Publishers Limited, 2008.

Sarich, Leah. *Frederiction: City of Stately Elms*. From the Canadian Cities series. Calgary: Weigl Educational Publishers Limited, 2002.

Lappi, Megan. *Canadian Sites and Symbols: New Brunswick*. Calgary: Weigl Educational Publishers Limited, 2004.

Tomljanovic, Tatiana. *Linking Canadian Communities: Forestry*. Calgary: Weigl Educational Publishers Limited, 2008.

WEBSITES

The Government of New Brunswick
www.gov.nb.ca

Outdoor Adventures in New Brunswick
www.out-there.com/newbruns.htm

Great Pictures of New Brunswick
www.tourismnbcanada.com/web/english

Some websites stay current longer than others. To find information on New Brunswick, use your Internet search engine to look up such topics as "Fredericton," "Bay of Fundy," "Saint John," or any other topic you want to research.

INDEX

Acadians 7, 29, 30, 31, 33, 36,
    37, 38, 39
aquaculture 19

Bay of Fundy 6, 8, 14, 15, 16,
    17, 43, 47
Bouctouche 6, 24, 38

Caraquet 23, 36
Carman, Bliss 38
Cartier, Jacques 26, 27
Chaleur Bay 6, 7, 13, 31
Champlain, Samuel de 26, 27
Colville, Alex 38, 39
Confederation 35, 44, 45

Dalhousie 7
dulse 14

Edmundston 23, 35, 39

fiddleheads 14, 46
forests 4, 6, 7, 11, 12, 13, 14,
    15, 19, 47
Fredericton 7, 8, 23, 32, 35,
    37, 38, 39, 42, 44, 46, 47
Fundy Isles 17
Fundy National Park 6, 7, 14,
    15, 16, 41, 47

King George III 7
Kouchibouguac National
    Park 7, 41

Loyalists 30, 31, 33, 36, 37

Maillet, Antonine 38
Maliseet 24, 25

Mary's Point 14
Mi'kmaq 24, 25
Miramichi 7, 37, 39, 40,
    43, 46
Moncton 17, 19, 23, 32, 33,
    39, 43, 46
Mount Carleton 8

Northumberland Strait 6,
    7, 24

puffin 15

Restigouche River 6, 7, 13, 40
Roberts, Charles G.D. 38

Saint John 7, 21, 23, 30, 32,
    33, 37, 38, 42, 43, 46, 47
Saint John River 7, 8, 16,
    19, 24

Theatre New
    Brunswick 39